PARADISE EMPTY

Hugo Mujica
PARADISE
EMPTY
POEMS 1983-2013

Selected, introduced & translated by
Katherine M. Hedeen &
Víctor Rodríguez Núñez

Arc
PUBLICATIONS
2015

Published by Arc Publications,
Nanholme Mill, Shaw Wood Road
Todmorden OL14 6DA, UK
www.arcpublications.co.uk

Design by Tony Ward
Printed by Lightning Source

978 1910345 14 6 (pbk)
978 1910345 15 3 (hbk)
978 1910345 16 0 (ebook)

Cover design: Tony Ward

ACKNOWLEDGEMENTS

The translators wish to thank Hugo Mujica for his trust
in their work. They, together with Arc Publications,
are also grateful to Argentina's Programa Sur
for generously funding this project.

Supported using public funding by
ARTS COUNCIL
LOTTERY FUNDED **ENGLAND**

This work is published within the framework of
"SUR" Translation Support Program of the Ministry of Foreign Affairs,
International Trade and Worship of the Argentine Republic /
Obra subsidiada en el marco del
Programa SUR del Ministerio de Relaciones Exteriores
y Culto de la Repúbica Argentina

Programa **Sur**

Arc Publications 'Contemporary Spanish-American Poetry' series
Series Editors: Katherine M. Hedeen & Víctor Rodríguez Núñez

CONTENTS

Biographical Notes / 158

Hugo Mujica began publishing his poetry in 1983, when Argentina had just emerged from a bloody military dictatorship, and initiated an arduous democratic reconstruction that has yet to be completed. The so-called Dirty War (1974-1983) was a systematic action taken by the state in which, to avoid legal complications, no one was killed, but "disappeared". The truth commission documented nine thousand cases, but said there could be many others unreported, while organizations that defend human rights, such as the legendary Mothers of the Plaza de Mayo, have claimed 30,000. They were mostly young people between 15 and 35, and not just guerrillas or militants of political and social organizations, but trade unionists, priests, intellectuals, lawyers defending political prisoners, human rights activists. The aim was to stop the powerful social and cultural movement that, since the mid-1960s, sought the transformation of Argentina, to end underdevelopment and dependence, to end the neocolonial condition.

The poetry that Hugo Mujica became a part of had suffered, like everything in Argentina, the devastating consequences of disappearance, exile, censorship. It was no longer the poetry that, until the mid-1970s, had proposed bringing together avant-garde aesthetics and political participation, and whose most prominent representative is Juan Gelman. Comparable trends like Enrique Molina's *surrealismo*, Edgar Bayley's *invencionismo*, and Joaquin Giannuzzi's *objectivismo* had also gone by the wayside. Even the *neo-vanguardismo* that arose in the early years of the dictatorship, with its distrust of history, culture and language, had vanished. As poetic activity had been virtually wiped out, the new poets did not have to challenge their predecessors, they simply did their thing. The scene became more heterogeneous than before, with several tendencies that at times differed and at others converged: the Neo-Baroque of Arturo Carrera, Nestor Perlongher,

11

Tamara Kamenszain, and *Xul* magazine, the Neo-Objectivism of Diana Bellessi, Daniel Samoilovich, and *Diario de Poesía*, and the Neo-Romanticism of Jorge Boccanera, Víctor García Redondo, and the magazine and publishing house, *Ultimo Reino*.

Hugo Mujica's poetry does not participate in any of the trends that develop in Argentina beginning in the early 1980s. In fact, one could say that it confronts each and every one them, of course implicitly, with the eloquence of silence, the gesture that distinguishes his brilliant discourse. The one commonality is that social intervention takes place in an untraditional way, through a shift from politics to ethics. Still, Mujica's work is rooted in a current of the southern country's poetry, established in the early twentieth century and crossing generations and historical circumstances: the poetry of thought. Those belonging to this tradition include Macedonio Fernández, Antonio Porchia, Jorge Luis Borges, Amelia Biagioni, Alberto Girri, Roberto Juarroz, Héctor Viel Temperley, and Alejandra Pizarnik. Yet the way Mujica materializes thought as poetry acquires a remarkable singularity, an indisputable personality. His obsessions are others; his ways are different; his dialogues have other references.

The interlocutors of Hugo Mujica's poetry become explicit in his numerous brilliant essays. Just consider some of the titles: *Origin and Destiny: From the memory of the Pre-Socratic Poet to the Hope of the Poet in Heidegger* (1987), *The Way of the Word* (1989), *The Initial Word: The Mythology of the Poet in Heidegger* (1996), *Arrow in the Mist: Identity, Word and Fissure* (1997), *Poetics of the Void* (2002), *The Nascent: Thinking the Creative Act* (2007), *The Passion According to Georg Trakl: Poetry and Atonement* (2009), *The Knowledge of Not Knowing: Desert, Kabbalah, Unbeing, and Creation* (2014). It is a vast spectrum, from Taoism to Catholicism, from Expressionism to Existentialism, and poetry is at the heart of it all. So, to say that Mujica is, by being a priest, a Catholic poet, is not only a sin of determinism but, above all, to limit his full scope. His poetry is religious but in the broadest sense, from the dark Latin root of that word, by its sincere desire to "reconsider" and "reconnect". And it's not fundamentally mystical, as would be expected from common sense; rather it's thought that goes beyond the borders of theology, of philosophy itself.

If one accepts that ever since Plato metaphysics has been, as Heidegger thought, the oblivion of being and the inevitable fall into nihilism, it could be said that Mujica's poetry is radically anti-metaphysical. His poetic subject never thinks alone and so is always considered fulfilled; what distinguishes it from the void, from nothingness, from death, is its relationship with otherness, with the other. It is born from the pain that is not its own, from an encounter, and transcends not as individual but as community. The I is a bridge, one is the house of the other, one is only no one, the I grows silent and the other speaks, and even beauty is always another. Consequently, what is denounced are metaphysical contraries, like outside and inside, fear and hope, reason and emotion, body and soul. Opposites exist, but dialectically, that is to say, they are excluded as they are taken on. It recognizes the existence of reality, that it is not chaotic but sacred, that it reverberates in words. It is against the void, fragmentation, uprooting, oblivion. And this dialectic gnosiology is complemented by an ontology where the mirage, the mirror as an allegory, the glance are questioned because ultimately they imprison; if there is a hero in this lyric it is the blind man.

Hugo Mujica began publishing poetry when he was over forty and perhaps that's why we are freed from a novice's babbling. In other words, since his first book he has produced mature work, where there are highs and lows as is to be expected, still it evolves serenely with no

13

need for qualitative leaps. By challenging solipsism, he distances himself from Romanticism; by not hiding the condition of reality's representation in his art, he moves away from Realism; by rejecting verbal luxury, he breaks free from Spanish American *modernismo*; by not prioritizing rupture over continuity, he leaves behind the Avant-garde. Arguably Mujica offers an essential poetry, beyond time and space if that were possible, where what is sought is the bareness of content and form. There is nothing more than what is needed in these poems, in terms of image, rhythm and language. Nor is there description, only interpretation; indeed, always with a heightened awareness that poetry is a lone language, sufficient and unnegotiable. Not coincidentally, Mujica's poetry is one of the best in Argentina, and one of the most renowned in the Spanish language today.

Katherine M. Hedeen & Víctor Rodríguez Núñez

from
BRASA BLANCA / WHITE EMBER
(1983)

6

cierro el puño
y golpeo,

cierro el puño,

para no ver la
                mano vacía

20

sólo la lluvia no es fragmento

y algún pájaro
blanco
dibujando gestos de
infinito

patria de alas
el desarraigo

lo asible de tu ausencia

26

mientras creo ser algo soy eso:
algo

6

I close my fist
and swing,

I close my fist

to not see my
             hand empty

20

only the rain is not a fragment

and some white
bird
etching gestures of
infinite

homeland of wings
the uprooting

the graspable of your absence

26

as long as I believe I am something I am that:
something

32

cada uno al borde
de cada uno

viajeros
perdidos entre tanto no partir

niños saludando trenes

o
en la playa
oteando hacia lo siempre lejos

hacia el llegar de toda partida

35

cerca

muy cerca
se refleja un ciego
sobre mi lágrima callada

cerca

más cerca
pongo mi lágrimas en sus ojos

para que podamos ver

32

each one at the edge
of each one

travellers
lost among so much not parting

children greeting trains

or
on the beach
glimpsing toward the always far off

        toward the arriving of every departure

35

close

so close
a blind man is mirrored
upon my silenced tear

close

closer still
I place my tear in his eyes

so we both can see

38

amanece
lila
entre grises chimeneas

humilde
resurrección
de cada noche

un posible volver a
crearlo todo

algo así
como un perdón

39

así,
como haciendo el amor
por la herida

¿no nacemos acaso
                desde el dolor ajeno?

38

it dawns
lilac
among grey smokestacks

humble
resurrection
of each night

a possible returning to
create it all

something akin
to a pardon

39

so,
like making love
through the wound

aren't we perhaps born
                from another's pain?

from

**SONATA DE VIOLONCELO Y LILAS /
SONATA OF CELLO AND LILACS**
(1984)

8

todo fue como siempre:
     abrí las manos y estabas

y todo fue como siempre
     por única vez

9

la ventana
y tus dos jazmines sobre mi mesa

y esta vez un pájaro,
     esta vez de carne y alas

11

y del otro lado de todo nada
o quizá, el reflejo de este mismo lado:
     nada.

los espejos cortan la vida

8

everything was like always:
                          I opened my hands and there you were

and everything was like always
                          just this once

9

the window
and your two jasmines on my table

and this time a bird,
                          this time in flesh and wings

11

and on the other side of everything nothing
or perhaps, the reflection of this same side:
                          nothing.

mirrors sever life

13

llueve,

semillas de agua siembran
verde en los muros

un gato salta techados
y una rosa blanca
                    enrojece el ocaso

17

y sigo de este lado
de la ventana

aquí, donde se estrellan pájaros
                    contra un alba de vidrio

23

viajante
de palabras brumas
apretando en la mano
un vidrio:

todo nace de un encuentro

13

it's raining,

seeds of water sow
green on the walls

a cat jumps rooftops
and a white rose
                reddens the sunset

17

and I'm still on this side
of the window

here, where birds shatter
                against a glass dawn

23

traveller
of misty words
clutching in his hand
a shard of glass:

everything is born from an encounter

24

cuando no hay muros
tampoco ecos

sólo lluvia
cayendo
hacia
siempre

sólo el mendigo durmiendo
sobre un banco

como sobre la palma del mundo

27

terco
el ventanal en la casa
del ciego

ver ensombrece la mirada

24

when there are no walls
no echoes either

only rain
falling
toward
always

only the beggar sleeping
on a bench

like on the palm of the world

27

stubborn
the picture window in the house
of the blind man

to see darkens the glance

29

faro de mar adentro
un vaso vacío

la garganta abierta
          y cielo adentro el mar

35

golpearé toda la noche
              el tambor de la noche,

toda la vida la puerta
de la vida
hasta que abra

hasta salir de tanto afuera

29

lighthouse out to sea
an empty glass

the open throat
          and sea out to sky

35

I will bang all night
              on night's drum,

all life on life's
door
until it opens

until I take my leave of so much outside

from
RESPONSORIALES / RESPONSORIALS
(1986)

1

soy puente sobre el que camino
caída en la que caigo

soy este lado del miedo:

        la desnudez todavía carne

2

golpeando la puerta
        de la casa vacía

no para que me abran,
        para escucharme llamado

12

en lo hondo no hay raíces,

        hay lo arrancado

1

I am the bridge over the one I walk
the fall where I fall

I am this side of fear:

        nakedness still flesh

2

knocking on the door
        of the empty house

not so they'll open for me,
            to hear me called

12

in the deep there are no roots,

           there is the weeded out

19

pido una tregua a este pulir espejos
detrás de cada iris,

pido ya no ser este no ser en carne propia

34

y todo es talar la vida
con la que quemamos todo,

la ofrenda
al holocausto de la memoria.

sé que nada de esto es,
¿pero cómo serlo sin todo esto?

35

escuchando la música
no el instrumento

siendo el pasar
no lo pasado

19

I ask for a truce to this polishing mirrors
behind each iris,

       I ask to no longer be this not being in my own flesh

34

and it's all felling life
          with it we burn it all,

the offering
to memory's holocaust,

I know it's nothing of this
       still how to be it if not for all this?

35

listening to music
      not the instrument

      being the passing
         not the past

cuando no quede más que lo que no queda
arrancaré la certeza a lo improbable:

tu espejo a mi propio nadie

when nothing more remains than what doesn't remain
I'll weed out certainty from the improbable:

your mirror to my very own nobody

from
ESCRITO EN UN REFLEJO / WRITTEN IN A REFLECTION
(1987)

4

parto en cuatro el cántaro vacío
con todo lo esperado

descorro las cortinas que nada
cubrían,

y todo lo que falta
                   es lo que desde siempre sobra

6

entre la raíz y la flor
me fue dado abrazar el tallo

tus espinas que no piden agua
                   me salvarán de las rosas

11

como ver el reflejo en la copa
de la que se bebe,

como verse hecho de sed:
                   de la sed de reflejarnos

4

I break in four the empty jug
with all the awaited

I draw back the curtains that concealed
nothing,

and everything that's missing
is what's always been more than enough

6

among root and blossom
I was granted to embrace the stem

your thorns unthirsty
will save me from the roses

11

like seeing our reflection in the cup
we drink from,

like seeing ourselves made of thirst:
the thirst to be reflected

43

20

mujeres arrodilladas tejen
con sus miedos
un manto para el dios desnudo

a palabras levanto el muro
            contra el que se vuelva eco
                        tanto callarse tuyo

32

me vestí para el banquete
y me dieron a mondar mis huesos

me desnudé para
las bodas
y me revistieron de escarchas

            ¿de qué avaricia soy el precio?

20

women kneeling weave
with their fears
a cloak for the naked god

with words I raise the wall
    against which so much falling silent of yours
                                    turns to echo

32

I dressed for the banquet
and they put me to pare my bones

I undressed for
the wedding
and they cloaked me in frosts

            of what greediness am I the price?

34

con el oído apretado
contra un caracol desierto

también el silencio es un mar drenado
       y las palabras los ríos
       de ese mismo vacío en los que vierto mi vida.

de tajos la red con que nos atrapa dios

45

como ser la sed desde otra garganta,
o la mirada
que no cabe en tus ojos.

¿cuándo leerás mis poemas
       dios de mi ceguera?

34

with my ear snug
against the deserted seashell

silence too is a sea drained
        and words rivers
           of the same void where I pour my life

slashed the net we are trapped with by god

45

like being thirst from another throat
or the glance
that won't fit in your eyes.

when will you read my poems
                god of my blindness?

from
PARAÍSO VACÍO / PARADISE EMPTY
(1992)

LUNA SOBRE LAS OLAS

Hay luna sobre las olas y en el viento un canto que nadie canta. Sobre la playa, con los ojos vendados, seis niños caminan cargando un ataúd abierto. Caminan mar adentro al paso del canto que nadie canta.

Sobre las olas se mece el féretro como una cuna vacía mientras se ahogan bajo las aguas los gritos que nadie escucha.

Hay luna sobre las olas.

EL DESIERTO DE CADA DÍA

En el desierto de cada día el viento borra las huellas de todas las caravanas, barre los pasos de dios en el paso de cada hombre, borra las huellas de todos ellos en el desierto de cada mundo.

En el desierto de cada vida hay una huella que nada borra: la del desierto de cada vida, la huella que el viento traza.

CICLO

Un ciego, en medio del desierto, cava con sus manos un pozo redondo: esculpe una imagen a semejanza de lo único que le fue dado ver.

Una tribu trashumante saca del pozo agua, sacia su sed,

50

MOON ON THE WAVES

There's moon on the waves and on the wind a song nobody sings. On the beach, blindfolded, six children walk carrying an open casket. They walk at sea to the beat of the song nobody sings.

On the waves rocks the coffin like an empty cradle while beneath the waters drown the cries nobody hears.

There's moon on the waves.

THE DESERT OF EACH DAY

In the desert of each day the wind erases the traces of all the caravans, sweeps away god's steps in the steps of each man, erases the traces of all those in the desert of each world.

In the desert of each life there's a trace nothing erases: the desert of each life's, the trace the wind traces.

CYCLE

A blind man, in the middle of the desert, digs with his hands a round well: sculpts an image like the only thing he was granted to see.

A migrating tribe takes water from the well, quenches

51

deja su andar. A su alrededor aran, siembran árboles, instalan sus tiendas, edifican ciudades e inventan ciencias para que los ciegos puedan ver.

Tiempo después (cuando la arena ya fue sepultada en muros), poderosas cavadoras ahondan el pozo y, uno a uno, arrojan allí a los ciegos penitentes que se niegan a abrir los ojos para no dejar de ver.

Las hojas de los árboles comienzan a secarse.

JUEGO DE NIÑOS

—Es por orfandad que la muerte mata a sus hijos— dijo como añorando no haber sido su propio parto, mientras se desnudaba, quitándose el vestido de raso blanco que había vestido otra niña.

—¿La muerte tiene hijos?—, preguntó extrañado el niño, repasando en vano todo lo que le habían enseñado los mayores.

—No, pero yo hablaba de la vida— aclaró la muerte, complacida de que los huérfanos la comprendieran, mientras se ponía la ropa que le iba sacando al niño.

Se acostó desnudo, cerró los ojos hasta soñar la completa oscuridad, tan oscura que ni la nieve se veía; apenas la sintió corriéndole lluvia por su cuerpo, como un vestido nuevo, como una transparencia negra.

its thirst, stops its wandering. All around they till, plant trees, put up tents, build cities and devise sciences so the blind can see.

Later on (when the sand was buried in walls), powerful diggers deepen the well, and one by one, throw there the blind penitents who refuse to open their eyes so to not stop seeing.

The leaves on the trees begin to wither.

CHILD'S PLAY

"It's by orphanage that death kills her children," she said as if yearning to not have been her own birth, while she unclothed, removing the white satin dress the other girl had worn.

"Does death have children?" asked the boy surprised, worthlessly going over everything the grown ups had taught him.

"No. But I was speaking of life," death clarified, pleased the orphans understood her, while she put on the clothes she took off the boy.

He lay down naked, closed his eyes until he dreamt of total darkness, so dark that even snow was unseen; he scarcely felt her running rain over his body, like new clothes, like a black translucence.

I

Tú hablas. Yo callo: digo un desierto a medida del infinito humano. Nos digo partidos por la mitad del otro.

– La página en blanco no busca ser escrita, pide ser leída –.

Dices, y callas: nosotros.

II

Habla, busca decirse para ser dicho por los otros, busca que los otros lo hagan semejante a él.

Habla de prisa para no terminar de hablar (para no saberse).

Callan, se desbarrancan, se abrazan. Miedo contra miedo: semejantes.

III

Dice que es sorpresa (no espanto).
Dice siempre lo que no puede decir, lo que todos dicen para no decir muerte.

Sonríe, saluda, todos saludan: mueren.
(Sin desesperar, sin haber esperado).

I

You speak. I fall silent: I utter a desert the size of the human infinite. I utter us split down the half of the other.

"The blank page doesn't want to be written, it asks to be read."

You utter and fall silent: we.

II

He speaks, wants to utter himself to be uttered by others, wants others to do so like him.

Speaks quickly so to not finish speaking (so to not know himself).

They fall silent, fling themselves, embrace. Fear against fear: fellows.

III

He utters it's surprise (not fright).
Utters always what he can't utter; what everyone utters to not utter death.

Smiles, greets, everyone greets: dies.
(No despair, no having waited.)

LEYES

Una rata se pudre ahogada dentro de un balde de agua; no lejos, un perro sigue atado desde que su amo partió.

A veces ladra, otras corre la distancia de la soga que no alcanza para llegar hasta el balde. (Cada vez se queda más tiempo echado. Hasta que no se levanta. Hasta que muere. Más de sed que de hambre).

En el balde, donde sigue pudriéndose la rata, el agua no termina de secarse.

LA ÚLTIMA GOTA

Los muertos suelen vestirse con nuestras sombras para seguir recorriendo las calles, para beber agua y no barro cuando la lluvia cae.

A la hora en que están encendidas las ciudades, como esas velas que siguen ardiendo en la noche de una iglesia cuando ya cerraron sus puertas, ahí están ellos, esperando que nos durmamos, esperando beber la última gota en la copa de vino que dejamos.

(Son ellos los que callan el silencio en el que nosotros hablamos; son ellos los que hablaron cuando a veces olvidamos lo que estuvimos soñando.)

LAWS

A rat rots drowned in a pail of water; not far away, a dog's been tied up since his owner left.

At times it barks, other times it runs the length of the rope that doesn't reach the pail. (Each time it lies down longer. Until it doesn't get up. Until it dies. More from thirst than hunger).

In the pail, where the rat's still rotting, the water refuses to dry out.

THE LAST DROP

The dead often dress in our shadows to keep on wandering the streets, to drink water and not mud when rain falls.

When the cities are lit up, like those candles that keep burning in a church night when its doors have already been shut, there they are, hoping we fall asleep, hoping to drink the last drop in the wine glass we leave behind.

(They're the ones who silent the silence we speak in; they're the ones who spoke when we at times forgot what we were dreaming.)

ECCE HOMO

Soñé con el llanto de otro hombre y desperté con el pecho devastado por la sal de su llanto: sediento y no bebí. Supe que debía abstenerme, sentir la sed como un verdugo siente la vida cada vez que la quita: ardiente. Sí, debía abstenerme, tragar doblemente el agua, la de mi sed y la del llanto del otro hombre: grano de sal sobre la lengua reseca.

Y esperar.
Hasta que la devastación me llegue a los ojos, hasta ser el hombre.

PALABRAS

(Todo ocurrió en palabras que no dicen lo que dicen ni el silencio que las dice, en palabras muertas, en las que la muerte va diciéndose mientras nos decimos, mientras nos habla para llegarnos a callar.)

I

Buscabas una, no todas, una palabra en la cual escucharnos, desde la cual llegarnos a decir; podría haber sido la palabra "fuente", pero no era "fuente" ni era una fuente en la que nadie se hubiera mirado: una fuente sin nombrar. Era la palabra que faltaba en cada historia leída, la que había quedado sin narrar en todas las historias escritas, era la ausencia que hacía del punto final de todos los libros una caravana infinita, un infinito punto de suspensión, un infinito suspendido en cada final.

ECCE HOMO

I dreamt of the cry of another man and awoke with my chest devastated by the salt of his cry: thirsty but I did not drink. I knew I ought to abstain, feel thirst like an executioner feels life each time he takes it: burning. Yes, I ought to abstain, twice swallow the water, my thirst's and the other man's cry's: grain of salt upon the parched tongue.

And wait.
Until the devastation gets to my eyes, until I am the man.

WORDS

(It all happened in words that don't utter what they utter, not even the silence that utters them, in dead words, in those death utters while we utter ourselves, while she speaks to us so we come to grow silent.)

I

You sought one, not all, one word to listen to us in, from where we come to utter, it could have been the word "fountain," but it wasn't "fountain," it wasn't even a fountain no one would have looked into: a fountain unnamed. It was the word missing in every story read, the one that had gone untold in all the stories written, it was the absence that had made the ending point of all the books an infinite caravan, an infinite suspension point, a suspended infinite in each ending.

II

Hablamos hasta la sed, hasta el grito en que callan los sedientos (el grito con que los náufragos tragan el agua que los traga), después callamos, pero tampoco fue el silencio (esa evasión de los que no hablan, eso que se evade cuando hablamos).

Buscábamos la palabra en forma de hueco de esa palabra en todas las palabras, el hueco que hace de toda palabra un eco de ese hueco. Buscabas —lo dijiste cuando ya llorábamos— la palabra que no dice nada, la que se dice ella misma en toda palabra que no la dice, en las que nos decimos para no llegarnos a nombrar.

PARAÍSO VACÍO

Sólo la serpiente no fue arrojada: permanece arrastrándose en círculos más y más cerrados, abriendo el infierno de un paraíso vacío. Gira en el vacío vaciando un círculo en el polvo: el hueco espejo del terco rito de ser el dios de mi propio infierno.

META

Es como si una lágrima hubiese perdido su senda y por error o errante, tal vez, hubiera hecho lago en mi alma.

60

We speak until thirst, until the cry where all the thirsty grow silent (the cry all the shipwrecked swallow the water that swallows them with), later we grew silent, still it wasn't the silence (that evasion of those who don't speak, what's evaded when we speak).

We sought the word in the shape of a hollow of that word in all words, the hollow that makes every word an echo of that hollow. You sought –you uttered it when we were already crying– the word that utters nothing, the one that utters itself in every word that does not utter it, in those we utter ourselves to not come to be named.

PARADISE EMPTY

Only the serpent was not thrown out: it lingers crawling in tighter and tighter circles, opening the hell of a paradise empty. It spins in the void emptying a circle in the dust: the mirrored hollow of the stubborn ritual of being god of my own hell.

AIM

It's as if a tear had lost its way and out of error or errant, perhaps, had become lake in my soul.

Es sal.

Y es menos que un nudo, más que una cuerda: un arco que suspende el aliento.

A veces, siempre de vez en vez, he tratado de llegar hasta allí para lavarme los ojos. Pero es tan lejos que antes encuentro el olvido y vuelvo a hacer casa en mi sombra hasta el próximo llanto; hasta que otra vez anhelo esa lágrima: la que me transparente el adentro.

La sal ya es diamante, o perla: estatua de sal de una fuente perdida.

Meta, para un arco sin flecha.

AUSENCIA

Fue cuando no pude más y grité "¡yo!", cuando escuché mi eco diciéndome "¡yo!".

Y supe que las cosas nunca habían tenido bordes, que el hueco de todas las bahías se recortaba en mí, que el borde de todos los otros comenzaba donde faltaba yo.

Fue cuando supe que no había nadie.

Pero no corrí de un lado a otro para encontrarme con nadie, me quedé solo y, aún así, alguien estaba de más. Quizás no era yo, era el eco de mí.

It's salt.
And it's less than a knot, more than a rope: a bow suspending breath.

At times, always from time to time, I've tried to reach there to wash my eyes. But it's so far off that beforehand I find oblivion and once more make my home in my shadow until the next cry; until I long for that tear again: the one that makes clear my inside.

Salt is now diamond or pearl: salt statue of a lost spring. Aim, for an arrowless bow.

ABSENCE

It was when I couldn't stand it anymore and yelled out "I!," when I heard my echo uttering to me "I!"

And I discovered things had never had edges, the hollow of all the bays were silhouetted against me, the edge of all the others began where I was missing.

It was when I discovered there was nobody.

But I didn't run around to meet up with nobody, I stayed by myself, and even still, someone was in the way. Perhaps it wasn't me, it was the echo of me.

Fue entonces cuando me asaltó una duda: si no había nadie ¿sobre quién rebotaba mi grito para volverse eco de mí?

(Es sobre esta duda que ahora escribo, o tal vez, sea sobre la misma esperanza que siempre escribí.)

That's when a doubt struck me: if there was nobody, who did my cry bounce off of to turn into an echo of me?

(It's about that doubt I now write, or perhaps it's about the same hope I always wrote.)

from
PARA ALBERGAR UNA AUSENCIA / TO HOUSE AN ABSENCE
(1995)

RITUAL DE LO INÚTIL

como ver caer
una estrella
sin nombrar un deseo;

o como a quien no se le destinó
ningún destino salvo
la espera
de lo que pasará
        sin llevarnos,

lo que miramos
sin ver
porque no es igual a nosotros.

ritual de lo inútil
o la esperanza extrema:

un niño ciego frente
a un espejo,
como si lo que uno es
        no hiciera falta para serlo.

HAY PERROS QUE MUEREN DE LA MUERTE DE SU AMO

hay perros
que mueren de la muerte de su amo

cuerpos que no hacen el amor,
hacen el miedo

RITUAL OF USELESSNESS

like glimpsing a falling
star
and not making a wish;

or like one who wasn't granted
any other destiny than
the waiting
for what will happen
                    if we're not taken along,

what we glance
not seeing
because it's not the same as us.

ritual of uselessness
or extreme hope:

a blind boy facing
a mirror
as if what one is
            isn't really necessary to be it.

THERE ARE DOGS THAT DIE FROM THE DEATH OF THEIR OWNERS

there are dogs
that die from the death of their owners

bodies that don't make love,
they make fear

que no se agitan,
       tiemblan.

y hay hombres
en los que muere dios
como una gota de lacre
sobre el pecho
       de un torso de mármol,

son los que lloran cuando creen
estar hablando,
o gritan soñando, pero al alba
olvidan el grito
con que encendieron la noche.

hay hombres en los que gime dios
por no encontrar un hombre
            donde morir de carne,

pero no llora como quien lo hace
solo,
llora como quien llora abrazado a un niño.

LA MISMA NOCHE, UN MISMO SUEÑO

cada uno cava en uno
       la casa del otro

el imposible hogar
de todo exiliado;

that do no shake,
        they tremble.

and there are men
in which god dies
like a drop of sealing wax
on the chest
        of a marble torso,

they are those who cry when they think
they're speaking
or cry out dreaming, but at dawn
they forget the cry
they lit up the night with.

there are men in which god howls
from not finding a man
                    where he can die from flesh,

but he doesn't cry like anyone who does it
alone,
he cries like someone cries embracing a child.

THE SAME NIGHT, A SAME DREAM

every one digs in one
            the other's house

the impossible home
of every exile;

cada otro nos pide la palabra
que no tenemos

la que diga lo que dice
sin decir despedida,

la esperanza de dar
lo que siempre hemos pedido.

unos y otros la misma noche,
cada noche
un mismo anhelo:

brindar chocando otra copa
                    sin que el cristal se nos quiebre.

EN LA NOCHE SOBRE LA PLAYA

hay lunas
que pintan de cal las noches,

noches en que el silencio
arde
mientras el viento
hace girar
cenizas en su rueda sin destino.

quedaría hacerse casa,
ordenar los escombros o cavar
en las cenizas
la imposible madriguera

every other asks us for the word
we don't have

the one that utters what it utters
without uttering goodbye,

the hope of giving
what we've always asked for.

ones and others the same night,
every night
a same longing:

to toast clinking another cup
                    without breaking the glass.

IN THE NIGHT ON THE BEACH

there are moons
that whitewash the nights

nights where silence
burns
while the wind
makes ashes
spin in their aimless wheel.

what would be left is to make a home,
order the rubble or dig
in the ashes
the impossible den

morder los labios
para probar el filo
            de los propios dientes

o elegir la mansedumbre
de cerrar los ojos
y esperar

como un caballo en la noche
tumbado
sobre la playa,

un caballo caído
            con la pata quebrada.

TIERRA QUEMADA

hay un monje arrodillando
su vida
en un sudario
en el que nadie
            jamás se ha secado.

una virgen que cose
con una aguja sin hebras
el traje
para sus bodas

y está todo hombre
cortándose las palmas de las manos
de tanto apretar los puños,

bite lips
to try out the edge
            of our very teeth

or opt for the meekness
of closing eyes
and waiting

like a horse in the night
stretched out
on the beach,

a horse fallen
            with a broken leg.

SCORCHED EARTH

there is an monk kneeling
his life
in a shroud
where nobody
            has ever withered.

a virgin who sews
with a threadless needle
the dress
for her wedding

and every man
slicing the palms of his hands
from so much squeezing of fists,

o abriéndolas como un náufrago
para hacer señas
                   a nadie.

hay el único desierto:
el no haber partido,
            el saber que no habrá llegada.

OTRO INICIO, OTRA MÚSICA

nada responde a nada
cuando todo habla.

hay que soñar
un sueño sin voces,

volver a cantar escuchando.

dejar correr una lágrima
con la cara
bajo la lluvia

un silencio
que sea anuncio, un anuncio
que lo nazca,

            un alba en la palabra alba.

or opening them like a castaway
to make signals
                to nobody.

there's the only desert:
the not having parted,
                the knowing there will be no arrival.

ANOTHER BEGINNING, ANOTHER MUSIC

nothing responds to nothing
when everything speaks.

one must dream
a voiceless dream,

sing once more listening.

let fall a tear
with face
beneath the rain

a silence
that's a sign, a sign
that bears it,

                a dawn in the word dawn.

LENTAMENTE

amparada en la noche
de una iglesia

una rata roe los pies
de la imagen
                del ángel.

afuera llueve
sobre un maniquí abandonado
en una plaza

lentamente
(como la lluvia cae)
se va disolviendo
                la trama.

bordeándolos se dibujan los abismos

borrando los bordes
                se abre la rosa.

PARA ALBERGAR UNA AUSENCIA

se nace para albergar
una ausencia
y la desterramos
                hacia horizontes,

SLOWLY

sheltered in the church
night

a rat gnaws at the feet
of the image
        of the angel.

outside it rains
on an mannequin abandoned
in a square

slowly
(like the rain falls)
the lines
        dissolving.

skirting them the abysses are drawn

erasing the edges
        the rose opens.

TO HOUSE AN ABSENCE

we're born to house
an absence
and we banish it
        toward horizons,

a veces somos nosotros esa
ausencia,
a veces osamos el frío
                    que otro cuerpo tiembla

o el hambre
que nos hace iguales.

sólo a veces,
como para saber qué fue
la vida

como para saber que fuimos otros.

at times we are that
absence,
at times we dare the cold
              another body trembles

or the hunger
that makes us equals.

only at times
as if to know what was
life

as if to know we were others.

from
NOCHE ABIERTA / NIGHT OPEN
(1998)

HAY UN ALMA

apenas la sed
descubre sin cubrir, apenas el agua
acaricia el borde
sin extender la herida,

es lo ausente lo que más
se muestra,
lo olvidado lo que más se espera.

hay un alma

lo dice la sed y
el agua

lo calla el olvido, la herida
abierta entre el sueño
y la vigilia

el naufragio de todo reflejo
                           en la transparencia olvidada.

ANTE NADA, PARA NADA

I

hay vidas que se consumen
                a través de una ventana,

mueren sin encontrar
un camino,
mueren de no haber partido.

THERE IS A SOUL

scarcely thirst
discovers not covering, scarcely water
caresses the edge
not spreading the wound,

the absent is what's
most shown,
the forgotten what's most awaited.

there is a soul

it's uttered by thirst and
water

it's silenced by oblivion, the open
wound between sleep
and wakefulness

the shipwreck of all reflection
$\qquad\qquad\qquad$ in the forgotten clarity.

BEFORE NOTHING, FOR NOTHING

I

there are lives consumed
$\qquad$ through a window,

they die not finding
a way,
they die from not having parted.

85

hay plegarias que son su propio eco;

esperanzas que son espejos:
aguardan
sólo lo que aguardan,
se transforman en la estatua
de aquello que esperaban,

son el miedo a perder
                    no el deseo del encuentro.

II

hay otras, otras vidas, que laten vida:
buscan
lo aún sin nombre
hacen del azar su esperanza,

no miran a lo lejos
                    hacen de la lejanía un atajo.

es la de hombres que hablan con palabras
que no son palabras
son golpes
contra el pecho de la vida,

como los que dan contra las paredes
los presidiarios
para que desde otra celda respondan.
son como mudos moviendo
los labios
dentro de una ronda de ciegos,

there are prayers that are their own echo;

hopes that are mirrors:
awaiting
only what they await,
shifting into the statue
of what they hoped for,

they are the fear of losing
                    not the desire for encounter.

        II

there are others, other lives, that pulse life:
seek
the still unnamed
turn fate to their hope,

don't look far off
                    turn distance to shortcut.

it is of men who speak with words
that are not words
they are blows
against the chest of life,

like knocks on walls
by prisoners
so another cell responds.
they are like the dumb moving
their lips
in a circle of blind men,

como mudos, sí,
pero sin cerrar la boca, sin traicionar el grito.

III

y hay vidas que ni gritan
ni golpean,
que no tienen ni siquiera una tapia donde
tatuar un nombre,
donde inscribir su paso,

son vidas a la intemperie: es la espera
en carne viva

como la de un mendigo en medio
de un páramo

ante nadie, para nada,
                    pero sin bajar ni cerrar la mano.

A VECES LA VIDA

a veces
nos miramos en silencio

la vida y yo.

a veces duele, duele
blanca,
lenta

like the dumb,
but mouth unclosed, not betraying the cry.

III

and there are lives that don't cry out
or give blows,
that don't even have a wall
to tattoo a name on,
to inscribe their passing,

they are lives out in the open: it is the waiting
in the raw flesh

like a beggar's in the midst
of a wasteland

before nobody, for nothing,
              yet with no lowering or closing the hand.

AT TIMES LIFE

at times
we watch each other in silence

life and me.

at times it hurts, hurts,
white,
slowly

se hunde en la carne
como una botella vacía se hunde en el
estanque
que la va llenando.

a veces, en silencio, llora
y algo sagrado brilla en el mundo,
        en silencio, reverbera en las palabras.

NOCHE ADENTRO Y NO DUERMO

a lo lejos, en un atardecer
en que el otoño
es un lugar en mi pecho,
comienzan a encenderse las ventanas,

mi nostalgia
por estar donde bien sé que al llegar
volvería a estar afuera.

duelen los ojos de soñar tan a lo lejos

la frente de pensar
lo impensable de tanta vida
que no he abrazado,
tanta deuda de lo que no he nacido.

poco a poco se apagan las luces,

it burrows in the flesh
like an empty bottle burrows in the
pond
filling it up.

at times, in silence, it cries
and something sacred shines in the world,
in silence, it reverberates in words.

DEEP IN NIGHT AND I CAN'T SLEEP

far off, on an evening
when autumn
is a place in my chest,
windows begin to light up,

my nostalgia
for being where I know for sure when I arrive
I would return to the outside.

my eyes hurt from dreaming so far off

my forehead from thinking
the unthinkable of so much life
I haven't embraced,
so much debt of what I haven't been born.

little by little the lights die down,

es el lindero de una noche y otra noche,
la frágil vecindad
    del miedo y la esperanza.

el último día podría ser éste que termina,
esta noche
en la que aún escribo

igual, pero sin una ausencia nueva
             para seguir esperando.

HASTA EL FINAL

vi un perro negro muerto
en la calle,
aplastado en medio de la acera, manchado,
porque nevaba.

vi la vida, allí mismo,
y no había más que eso: la coartada
del inocente: pagarlo todo.

sentí en la nieve la vida y me vi morir
como un animal que se resiste
hasta lo último

hasta el deseo de ser rematado,

hasta el gemido final,
el que pide perdón por todo crimen ajeno:
            el que perdona a dios.

it is the boundary between one night and another night,
the fragile surroundings
             of fear and hope.

the last day might be this one that's ending,
this night
where I still write

the same, and yet with not one new absence
                              to keep up the wait.

UNTIL THE END

I saw a dead black dog
on the street,
crushed in the middle of the sidewalk, stained,
from the snow.

I saw life, right there,
and there was nothing more than this: the innocent's
alibi: to pay for it all.

I felt life in the snow and I saw myself die
like an animal withstanding
until the end

until the desire to be finished off,

until the final cry,
the one asking for forgiveness for all the crimes of others:
                              the one forgiving god.

SIN SOMBRAS NI HUELLA

hay que caminar descalzo,
huir desnudo
como un fugitivo sin meta
                    para no estar nunca perdido.

    hundirse como una brasa
    en la nieve,

o caer
como cae la lluvia para ser lluvia,
caer sin más huella
            que esa misma caída.

hundirse, caer
o volar como vuela de desnudez el viento
huyendo del espejo
            que nos atrapa en cada llegada.

HACE APENAS DÍAS

hace apenas días murió mi padre,
hace apenas tanto.

cayó sin peso,
como los párpados al llegar
la noche o una hoja
cuando el viento no arranca, acuna.

hoy no es como otras lluvias
hoy llueve por vez primera
                sobre el mármol de su tumba.

NO SHADOWS OR TRACE

one must walk barefoot,
flee naked
like a drifting fugitive
                    to not ever be lost.

sink like an ember
in the snow,

or fall
like the rain falls to be rain,
to fall with no more trace
                    than that very falling.

to sink, to fall,
or to fly like the wind flies from nakedness
fleeing the mirror
                    that snares us in every arrival.

ONLY A FEW DAYS AGO

only a few days ago my father died,
only a few so many.

he fell weightless,
like eyelids when night
arrives or a leaf
when the wind doesn't uproot but cradles.

today is not like other rains
today it's raining for the first time
                    over the marble of his grave.

bajo cada lluvia
podría ser yo quien yace, ahora lo sé,
> ahora que he muerto en otro.

ATARDECE

es la hora en la que el vivir duda.

una línea en sesgo dibuja
sobre la medianera
de un edificio
la frontera entre el día y su sombra

la avidez y el abatimiento.

ni más allá ni más acá: ni dios ni
yo, sólo márgenes,
líneas

fatiga de nombrar los afueras
de cada nombre

cornisas y umbral hacia lo que calla,
lo que sólo el fracaso, a veces,
> en algún atardecer, escucha.

al comienzo se busca
lo alto, después, caída a caída,
> se muere raíces.

beneath each rain
it could be me lying there, now I know,
                    now that I've died in another.

TWILIGHT

is the hour when living doubts.

a diagonal line sketches
on a building's
sidewall
the border between day and its shadow

greed and dejection.

not further not nearer: not god not
me, only edges,
lines

fatigue from naming the outskirts
of each name

ledges and threshold to what silences,
what only failure, at times,
            in some evening, hears.

in the beginning what's sought
is the highness, later, fall after fall
                        the roots die.

from
SED ADENTRO / AT THIRST
(2001)

RELÁMPAGO

El relámpago y sus huellas:
        las cenizas en la memoria
            (el instante y su ceguera blanca).

Toda sombra es ayer,
        la belleza es siempre otra.

UNA VEZ MÁS

Después del relámpago es otra
        la misma noche:

      es que todo es lo que es y también
           una vez más

UNO TRAS OTRO

Se escribe cerrando
los ojos,

palabra tras
      palabra,

como caminan uno tras otro
los ciegos
sobre los charcos:
      sin mirarse en los reflejos.

LIGHTNING

Lightning and its traces:
                    ashes in memory
                              (instant and its white blindness).

All shadow is yesterday,
                    beauty is always other.

ONCE MORE

After lightning is another
                         the same night:

            for everything is what it is and too
                                        once more.

ONE AFTER ANOTHER

We write closing
our eyes,

word after
            word,

like the blind walk
one after another
over puddles:
        not seeing themselves in the reflections.

101

Se escribe
como se muere o se olvida
perdiéndose en la búsqueda,

    no en su eco: en lo que buscamos

DONDE ME DIGO

En lo alto no se baten
las alas
ni en el silencio
se nombra al silencio.

De dios no sabemos nada

esa nada hiende
todo saber,
esa hendidura es lo aprendido

la ausencia que queda,
           la huella donde me digo.

We write
like we die or forget
going astray in the quest,

not in its echo: in what we seek.

WHERE I UTTER MYSELF

In the heights wings
don't flap
and in the silence
silence isn't named.

We know nothing of god

that nothing splits
all knowing,
that split is what's learned

the absence remaining
the trace where I utter myself.

UN CIRIO EN LA PLAYA

I

Un cirio hendido en la playa.

> *(Una frágil soledad; una vigilia:*
> *un velar nada.)*

A veces, el viento sopla y la llama cambia su forma,
dibuja un gesto
como una despedida, o como quien llega y
se anuncia.

> *(El que sueña*
> *ya no es el mismo que el que duerme*
> *ni es igual la misma noche.)*

II

Un cirio apagado,
            la soledad de nadie.

(El hueco que cada muerte deja,
            la playa, que cada muerto cava.)

EL ANUNCIO

Raro relámpago del
instante,

brilla y ciega sobre
            un plato blanco y vacío.

AN ALTAR CANDLE ON THE BEACH

I

An altar candle split open on the beach.

(A fragile solitude; a vigil:
a watch over nothing.)

At times the wind blows and the flame changes shape,
sketches a sign
like a farewell, or one arrived and
announced.

(The one who dreams
is no longer the same as the one who sleeps,
very night is not equal.)

II

An altar candle snuffed out,
solitude of no one.

(The hollow each death leaves,
the beach dug by each of the dead.)

THE SIGN

Strange lightning bolt of
the instant,

glows and blinds above
an empty white plate.

Hay que acoger el fulgor de la ausencia,

reflejar
el don de lo que no está
                    en cada cosa que creamos.

DESPUÉS, LETRA A LETRA

Luna
entre los campanarios de una iglesia.

También los caminos huyen y, a veces, el cuerpo
                              miente sus sombras.

    I

Al principio todo fue blanco, blanco luna (la desnudez de
    un cuerpo
sin nombre), después, letra a letra,
la escritura

(y la sombra de las palabras:
                    el camino de narrar la noche).

We must embrace the gleam of absence,

reflect
the gift of what is not there
                              in everything we create.

LATER, LETTER BY LETTER

Moon
between a church bell towers.

The paths flee too, and at times, the body
                              fibs its shadows.

    I

In the beginning all was white, moon white (the nakedness
    of a nameless
body), later, letter by letter,
writing

(and the shadow of the words:
                    the path to narrate the night).

II

La muerte
es la ausencia de la palabra muerte. *Como al principio,*
como la desnudez,

    como sin decirme yo.

   (III
La ausencia no sólo calla:
               también bautiza.)

II

Death
is the absence of the word death. *Like in the beginning
like nakedness,*

    like without uttering myself.

  (III

The absence not only silences:
                    it too baptizes.)

from
CASI EN SILENCIO / ALMOST IN SILENCE
(2004)

LO AJENO

Sobre el muro,
inmóvil,
un gato dilata sus pupilas hacia
                              la noche.

Brillan ojos y luna,

y yo aquí,
ciego,
cuento lo que no veo:
                  digo la luz ajena.

TRANSPARENCIA

Noche sin cielo
y lo más alto
            es el nacer de la lluvia.

Sin un antes
ni un después,
        en su puro ahora

cae la lluvia;

cae sobre el mundo
y algo,
algo otro que la duda o la certeza,
                        se transparenta sobre sus aguas.

THE OTHER

On the wall
unmoving,
a cat dilates its pupils toward
                            night.

Glow eyes and moon,

and I am here,
blinded,
tell what I don't see:
                utter the other light.

CLARITY

Night skyless
and what's highest
                is the birthing of rain.

With no before
or after
    in its absolute now

the rain falls;

falls over the world
and something,
something other than doubt or certainty,
                        turns clear upon its waters.

EN LO OSCURO

Brisa, y
ondean los árboles,

el olor del tilo dice al tilo
                    en medio de lo oscuro.

Los que fueron ya regresaron,
duermen.

En la noche,
solitario, lo que nace habla,
                    lo que va muriendo escucha.

ENTRE LA NOCHE Y EL ALBA

Entre el tejado y el cielo

hay un vacío de
pájaros,

una nostalgia de lluvias.

Entre la noche y
el alba

la cita imposible de cada vida:
                    la ausencia que el alma abraza.

IN THE DARK

Breeze, and
trees flutter,

the scent of Tilia utters to Tilia
                        at dark's midpoint.

Those who left have now returned,
they are sleeping.

In the night,
solitary, what is born speaks,
                        what is dying listens.

BETWEEN NIGHT AND DAWN

Between roof and sky

there is a void of
birds,

a nostalgia of rains.

Between night and
dawn

impossible gathering of every life:
                        absence the soul embraces.

CAUCES

Sopla el viento
sobre lo oscuro de
                este invierno;

sopla y pasa como un río
que pasando creara
                él mismo sus orillas.

Siempre hay alguien que
se arrodilla
        en la noche,

alguien en quien la espera
                se le abre alma en la carne.

INFANCIA

Llueve
y al árbol le pesan sus hojas,
                a los rosales sus rosas.

Llueve
y el jardín huele a infancia,

a cercanía de todos los milagros,
                a ausencia de todas las memorias.

RIVERBEDS

The wind wafts
over the dark of
        this winter;

wafts and blows like a river
flowing crafts
        its own shores.

There is always someone to
kneel down
     in the night,

someone where the wait
        opens up soul in the flesh.

CHILDHOOD

It rains
and the tree is weighed down by its leaves,
        the rose bushes their roses.

It rains
and the garden smells of childhood,

nearness of all miracle,
        absence of all memory.

LLUVIA SOBRE LLUVIA

Al fondo,
sobre una mesa, debajo de
                              un árbol desnudo,

una taza
desborda la lluvia.

Desborda, cae, y dibuja un charco,
                              un espejo, una vida.

COMO EL MAR

Como el mar,

como su derramarse
playas
para permanecer en sí mismo,

así el alma
              en la vida,

pero sin albas
ni estrellas que se reflejen

sin luz alguna que
              ciegue su transparencia.

RAIN ON RAIN

In the background,
on a table, beneath
                a bare tree,

a cup
spills the rain.

It spills, falls, traces a puddle,
                        a mirror, a life.

LIKE THE SEA

Like the sea,

like its overflowing
beaches
to linger in itself,

so the soul
            in life,

yet with no dawns
or stars to reflect

no single light to
            blind its clarity.

UNA ESTRELLA

Anochece
      y se va apagando la arena.

Un pescador, todavía niño, dormita
      en un bote varado;

levemente la soledad lo cubre,
      su soledad del mundo y la primera estrella.

HENDIDURA

Sobre un mudo azul
el viento deshilacha nubes;

un pájaro atraviesa
el cielo

abre y cierra un instante,
      hiende mi mirada.

Pasa y desaparece hacia más allá que ver,
      hacia lo que jamás se olvida.

A STAR

Night falls
       and sand dies down.

A fisherman, still a boy, naps
             on a stranded boat;

solitude covers him slightly,
         his solitude of the world and the first star.

SPLIT

Upon a muted blue
the wind fraying clouds;

a bird crosses
the sky

opens closes an instant,
            splits my glance.

Flies by and disappears beyond the seeing,
            toward what is never forgotten.

ABANDONO

Entre el puño
   y la mano que se abre
         se despliega una vida.

Sólo la muerte no nos es ajena,
      sólo lo más propio nos nace del abandono.

REFLEJO

Atardece
y el murmullo del río
      dice al silencio del río.

Hay que mirar pasar
el agua
hasta ver tan sólo
      el paso del agua,

hasta ver en su transparencia
      el reflejo de la propia ausencia.

A LO LEJOS

A lo lejos,
más allá del camino,

se lee el viento
    en el humo inclinado.

ABANDON

Between fist
      and hand opening
            unfolds a life.

Only death is not other to us,
          only what is most ours is born of abandon.

REFLECTION

It twilights
and the river's murmur
        utters to the river's silence.

We must watch the flow
of water
until only seeing
        the water's flow,

until seeing in its clarity
        the reflection of absence itself.

FAR OFF

Far off,
beyond the path,

wind is read
      in the slanting smoke.

A lo lejos, pero sin salir,
        donde la lejanía es adentro
                donde un soplo me abre otro.

POÉTICA

Un relámpago,
        en la noche que dilata,
                alumbra su mismo apagarse.

ANUNCIO

Atardece otoño,

viento
y, de tanto en tanto, alguna hoja surca
                mi ventana;

de tanto en tanto, algo se anuncia
        en la indecisa belleza de
                cada hoja que cae.

Far off, but not leaving,
      where distance is within
           where one breath of air opens me another.

POETICS

A lightning bolt,
      in the dilating night,
           flashes its very fading.

SIGN

It twilights autumn,

wind
and, from time to time, some leaf scores
           my window;

from time to time, something is signaled
           in the undecided beauty of
              every falling leaf.

from
**Y SIEMPRE DESPUÉS EL VIENTO /
AND THE WIND ALWAYS AFTER**
(2011)

(CONFESIÓN

El poema, el que anhelo,
al que aspiro,
es el que pueda leerse en voz alta sin que nada se oiga.

Es ese imposible el que comienzo cada vez,
                es desde esa quimera
                          que escribo y borro.)

REGRESO

Hay que adentrarse
en el desierto
        para dejar atrás los espejismos;

hay que volver
a embriagarnos en la fuente:
                hay que regresar a la sed.

EN LA PIEL

A lo lejos, afuera,

        cae
        una lluvia
        que tan sólo huelo, una lluvia
                que aún no ha llegado.

(CONFESSION

The poem, the one I long for,
the one I aspire to,
is one to be read aloud without hearing a thing.

It's this impossibility I begin each time,
          it's from that chimera
                              I write I erase.)

RETURN

We've got to go deep
into the desert
          to leave the mirages behind;

we've got to go back
to revel in the fountain:
                    we've got to return to thirst.

ON THE SKIN

Far off, outside,

          falls
          a rain
          only I can breathe in, a rain
                              yet to appear.

Aquí
en la piel, como en una página
en blanco,
espero que el agua, la lluvia,
                    lo que vive y tiembla
                              me sea alguna vez revelado.

CADA VIDA

Una tras otra se alzan y
caen las olas
y ni tan sólo una gota le quitan
                              ni una gota le agregan al mar;

así cada vida a la vida:

                    cada instante de espuma
                              sobre esta playa con sed.

NACE EL DÍA

Nace el día
bajo un cielo despejado,

          la claridad en la que todo
          se muestra,
          lo que hacia ella brota
                    y lo que su misma luz marchita.

Here
on the skin, like on a blank
page,
I wait for the water, the rain,
        what lives and flutters,
                to one day be revealed to me.

EACH LIFE

One after the other waves rise
and fall
and not one drop do they rid
                not one do they add to the sea;

and so each life to life:

            each instant of sea foam
                    upon this thirsty beach.

DAY IS BORN

Day is born
beneath a cloudless sky,

        the clarity where all
        is shown,
        what springs toward it,
                and what its very light withers.

Todo nacer pide desnudez,
   como la pide el amor,
         como la regala la muerte.

TODO

Anochece rojo brasas,

         anochece
               y pasa el viento,

pasa sobre el llano
         que se abre noche,
               que se despliega vientos.

Todo cabe en las manos vacías
         y ese vacío es el don
               y ese don es también todo.

OFRENDA

Alguna vez,
cuando llegue a estar vacío,
         cerraré la puerta y arrojaré
               la llave;

Every birthing asks for bareness,
        just as love does,
                just as death grants.

ALL

Night falls red embers,

            night falls
                    and the wind wafts,

wafts over the plain
                    unfolding into night,
                            spreading into winds.

It all fits in empty hands
                and the emptiness is the gift
                        and the gift is all of it too.

OFFERING

One day,
when I end up empty,
            I'll close the door and toss out
                                the key;

sí,
habría que arrojarse afuera
como una ofrenda sin retorno,
como un regalo que nadie acoja.

AÚN NO

Agitar las alas todavía no es volar,
aún no es afuera.

Cuando el alma cabe por dentro
es que aún no es el alma,
es que aún no es de carne.

DESPUÉS DE TANTO

Después, después de tanto,
el miedo se pierde
al renunciar a lo que jamás se tuvo:

soy mi victoria sobre lo que perdí,
soy lo que ya no espero.

yes,
I'll have to toss myself out
            like an offering with no return
                        like a gift no one welcomes.

STILL NOT

To flap wings is not yet flying,
                        it's still not outside.

When the soul fits within
            it's still not soul,
                        it's still not made of flesh.

AFTER SO MUCH

Afterward, after so much
fear's lost
            once you renounce what was never had:

I am my victory over what I lost,
                        I am what I no longer await.

EN LO ALTO

Hay brisa

y una línea de álamos
acuna
la vastedad
de este anochecer
sobre el valle.

En lo alto
un pájaro aquieta
sus alas,

en lo alto, muy alto,
deja de apoyarse en su vuelo.

LA ORILLA

Tiembla una rama,
tiemblan sus últimas hojas
entre la luna y el agua.

No hay otro lado,
saberlo es el otro lado.

UP HIGH

There's a breeze

and a line of poplars
rocks
the vastness
of this nightfalling
over the valley.

> Up high
> a bird quietens
>   its wings,

up high, so high,
            stops leaning on in flight.

THE SHORE

A branch trembles,
its last leaves tremble
                among moon and water.

                There is no far side
                        knowing it is the far side.

CARNE VIVA

Sólo lo desnudo
no se pliega
        en sus bordes,

como un cielo abierto,
el alba

o un árbol
que fuese raíz
        en cada una de sus ramas,

o como una vida
        cuando es la carne viva
                de su propia nada.

SIN OÍRNOS

El sol declina
y la noche se anuncia
        serenando las voces;

queda llegar hasta un silencio
jamás nombrado,
        no para decirlo,
            para escuchar sin oírnos,
                para acoger el olvido.

RAW FLESH

Only the naked
won't bend
      at the edges,

like an open sky,
the dawn

or a tree
that would be root
      in each of its branches,

or like a life
    when it's the raw flesh
        of its own nothingness.

WITHOUT HEARING US

The sun declines
and night makes itself known
      hushing the voices;

what's left is to get to a silence
never named,
    not to utter it,
      to listen without hearing us,
        to welcome oblivion.

EN SÍ MISMA

Siempre
titubea una luz
que sólo se ve cuando
        no enciende nada,

como una desnudez
      que se revelara en sí misma,
          no en los ojos de quien la mira.

MÁS HONDO

Hay vidas
en las que el alma
      se abre
      más hondo
      que donde esas vidas laten,

se abre como un relámpago
sin cielo ni trueno,

     como una herida sin pecho

        o un abismo
          donde la belleza es alba.

IN ITSELF

Always
wavers a light
only seen when
        it gleams nothing,

like a bareness
        to be revealed in itself,
                not in the eyes of one who watches.

DEEPER

There are lives
where the soul
            opens
            deeper
            than where those lives pulse,

opening like a lightning bolt
no sky or thunder,

        like a chestless wound

                or an abyss
                        where beauty is dawn.

from
CUANDO TODO CALLA / WHEN IT ALL GOES QUIET
(2013)

II

Se enciende
el día sobre la desnudez
                de los llanos

        la neblina disuelve
        su velo
        y los sauces
                emergen renacidos.

Todo se abre y el verlo
                abre el alma,
                el alma que es ese abrirse.

        (El paraíso no fue perdido
                lo perdido es el asombro.)

III

Contra los acantilados
estallan ruidosas
        las olas,
                después regresan al mar,
                        vuelven
                                sin haberse separado.

Ningún fuego quema
        sus cenizas,
                ni por mucho andar
                        queda atrás el umbral
                                del que partimos.

II

Gleams
the day over the bareness
              of the plains

       mist dissolves
       its veil
       and the willows
                     arise reborn.

All of it opens and the seeing it
              opens the soul,
                     the soul which is that opening.

              (Paradise was not lost
                     what's lost is the wonder.)

III

Against the cliffs
stridently boom
              the waves,
              later they go back to the sea,
                            return
                                   with no parting.

              No fire burns
                     its ashes,
                            and despite great wandering
                                   no lingering behind for the threshold
                                   we leave from.

V

Inasible
una brisa roza la rama,
      las pocas vainas
           que cuelgan
                ondean su paso.

   Nada termina de comenzar
            ni jamás algo concluye,

                  tampoco lo que sin estar
                      deja de crearnos.

VI

Hay una hendidura
en la palabra
     hendidura,

un desgarro donde
              cada palabra calla,
                 donde todo callar crea;

es lo que en el decir es aliento
no de sonido
es donde en cada palabra
                nos escuchamos revelados.

v

Ungraspable
a breeze brushes the branch,
                the few husks
                        hanging
                                flutter its path.

Nothing finishes beginning
                and something never ends,

                        neither does what without being
                                ceases to create us.

VI

There's a split
in the word
        split,

a break where
        each word quiets,
                where all quieting creates;

it's what in the uttering is breath
not of sound,
it's where in each word
                we hear ourselves revealed.

VII

Hacia lo alto, hacia la luz
        se distancian las ramas,

        en lo hondo,
            en la oscura tierra,
                las raíces se encuentran,
                    la sed las entrelaza.

        X

Cuando la lejanía
late adentro
        es que el adentro
            ya es afuera;

    es haber llegado al alma,
            a ese hueco de nadie
                que en cada uno se abre todos.

    XX

A toda lluvia
la dicen sus gotas
        y la música con que cae,

VII

Toward highness, toward the light
                the branches drift apart,

                in the depths,
                    in the dark earth,
                        the roots converge,
                            thirst entangles them.

    X

When distance
pulses within
            the within
                    is now outside;

        it's having gotten to the soul,
                    that no man's hole
                        where in each one all open.

    XX

All rain
is uttered by its drops
                and the music it falls with,

a los rostros sus marcas
        y al silencio el mar
    cuando brama mar
            y la oveja
                cuando bala oveja.

        (No es que el silencio calle,
                lo que no deja es ecos:
                    lo que dice
                        dice siempre lo irrepetible.)

XXI

Se acuesta el sol
            y todo parece en vilo
                    como para revelar anunciar
                                un secreto.

            No basta con cerrar
            los labios,
                al silencio hay que escucharlo,
                        dejar que nos diga él
                                lo que de nosotros callamos.

faces by their scars
      and silence by the sea
    when it bellows sea
        and the lamb
           when it bleats lamb.

  (It's not that silence goes quiet,
      what it doesn't leave is echoes:
      what it utters
        forever utters the unrepeatable.)

XXI

Sun lies down
    and it all seems on edge
        like about to reveal signal
           a secret.

  It's not enough to seal
  our lips,
    we've got to listen to the silence
      let it utter to us
        what of ourselves we quiet.

XXII

Algunas huellas
     no son de pasos
          son de ausencias,
               no trazan, borran;

             son el atajo hacia el final,
               son las que nos salvan
                    del regreso.

XXVI

No toda raíz
cumple
su destino de luz
          ni cada grieta
             abre su promesa
               de abismo;

tampoco todo
andar
llega a palpar la tierra:
          apenas uno que otro
             entra descalzo a la muerte.

XXII

Some traces
      are not from steps
           but from absences,
                don't trace, erase;

                they are short cuts to the finish,
                    what saves us
                        from the return.

XXVI

Not every root
fulfills
its destiny of light
           not every crevice
                opens its promise
                    of abyss;

not every
wandering
comes to handle the earth:
           hardly anyone
                enters death barefoot.

XXVIII

El día no es solo día
también es
        noche encendida,
                sombra trasparentada.

    Es porque no tiene sombras
            que no vemos lo que el vacío enciende,
            que no vislumbramos
                    lo que nos queda
                            cuando no nos queda nada.

XXXIII

También el silencio
es huella,
        huella y seña
                hacia lo sin nombre

        hacia lo que solo
                        se escucha
                                en la renuncia
                                        a nombrarlo.

XXXIV

Más allá no es un lugar
                        ni uno mismo
                                es lo mismo que uno;

154

XXVIII

Day is not just day
it's also
     night gleamed
          shadow shown through.

Because it has no shadows
          we don't see what the void sets burning,
               we can't make out
                    what we have left
                         when all we have left is nothing.

XXXIII

Silence too
is trace,
     trace and sign
          toward the nameless

     toward what's only
                    heard
                         in the renouncing
                              once it's named.

XXXIV

Beyond is not a place
                    and one and the same
                         is not the same as one;

frente al espejo
no se viven dos vidas:
se repite la de nadie.

XL

Fugaz,
como el arco iris
que enciende
se abre el agua tras la proa;

se abre en dos
y son dos la misma agua.

XLVII

Siempre hay algo
que no llega a volverse carne:
no es que nos falte
es que nos excede.

La vida no cabe en la vida
por eso siempre,
en algún lugar, se nos parte.

facing the mirror
  we don't live two lives:
    nobody's is repeated.

XL

Fleeting
like the rainbow
    gleaming
      parts the water behind the prow;

        parted in two
          and two the very water.

XLVII

There's always something
    that doesn't end up turning to flesh:
      it's not that we're lacking
          it surpasses us.

      Life doesn't fit in life
        so always
          somewhere, it breaks on us.

157

HUGO MUJICA (b. Buenos Aires, 1942) is one of Argentina's top intellectuals and one of the leading poets in the Spanish language. At the age of thirteen, he began working at a glass factory, taking over for his father, who was blinded in a work accident. Ten years later, in the early sixties, he arrived in the USA and spent the decade in Greenwich Village and at the Free University, studying and practising the visual arts. He later became a Trappist monk and took a seven-year vow of silence. He has been a Catholic priest for more than two decades.

Mujica's work is wide-ranging, covering philosophy, anthropology, fiction, and poetry. His award-winning verse, made up of more than twenty volumes, has been published in fifteen countries. In 2013, Vaso Roto, one of the Spanish-speaking world's most prestigious presses, published his *Complete Poetry, 1983-2011*. That same year, he won Spain's coveted Casa de América Poetry Prize with *Cuando todo calla*.

Paradise Empty: Poems 1983-2013 in a bilingual edition offers the English-speaking reader for the first time a representative selection of all of Mujica's poetry, where idea and feeling, synthesis and eloquence, truth and beauty come together.

VÍCTOR RODRÍGUEZ NÚÑEZ (1955) is one of Cuba's most outstanding contemporary writers. He has published thirty books of poetry throughout Latin America and Europe, and has received major awards all over the Spanish-speaking world. Book-length translations of his work have been published in Chinese, German, English, French, Italian, Macedonian, Serbian and Swedish, and a wide selection of his poems has appeared in another twelve languages. He divides his time between Gambier, Ohio, where he is Professor of Spanish at Kenyon College, and Havana, Cuba.

KATHERINE M. HEDEEN is Professor of Spanish at Kenyon College. Her book-length translations include published collections by Rodolfo Alonso, Juan Bañuelos, Juan Calzadilla, Marco Antonio Campos, Luis García Montero, Juan Gelman, Fayad Jamís, José Emilio Pacheco, Víctor Rodríguez Núñez, and Ida Vitale. She is a two-time recipient of a National Endowment for the Arts Translation Project Grant.

ARC PUBLICATIONS
publishes translated poetry in bilingual editions
in these additional series:

ARC TRANSLATIONS
Series Editor Jean Boase-Beier

'VISIBLE POETS'
Series Editor Jean Boase-Beier

ARC CLASSICS:
NEW TRANSLATIONS OF GREAT POETS OF THE PAST
Series Editor Jean Boase-Beier

ARC ANTHOLOGIES IN TRANSLATION
Series Editor Jean Boase-Beier

NEW VOICES FROM EUROPE & BEYOND
(anthologies)
Series Editor Alexandra Büchler

details of which can be found on the
Arc Publications website at
arcpublications.co.uk